A Sip Of Hope

A Poet's Journal

Alyssa Eva

A Sip Of Hope
A Poet's Journal

ALYSSA EVE

A Sip Of Hope: A Poet's Journal
ALyssa Eve
Copyright © 2022 ALYSSA EVE. All rights reserved.
Published by ALYSSA EVE / FITTING TITLES
ISBN 978-1-716-06747-1

No part of this publication may be reproduced, stored or transmitted in any form or by any means, electronic, mechanical, photocopying, recording, scanning, or otherwise without written permission from the publisher. It is illegal to copy this book, post it to a website, or distribute it by any other means without permission.

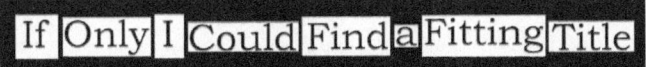

ALyssaEveBlando@gmail.com
FittingTitles@gmail.com

Find more books at: LULU.COM/SPOTLIGHT/ALYSSAEVE

December 2020

Of Gone For Good
Friday, December 25, 2020

Peace is an object I'm trying to obtain.
Leave me to my own devices,
and I'll find it in the rain.

A deep breath, I place my focus on my senses.
I can touch the silence like a breezy beach day.

Sand covers my feet
with a brand of warmth
which can't be beat.

Solace- I saw Him in a windowsill,
bright as God can shine.
I peaked out to see hope in the daylight,
opened it up to breathe in the vibrant air.

It's terrible we can't live without a care,
or pray our worries into an endless abyss.

Finding Grace

Sunday, December 27, 2020

Genuineness is not difficult to see
in the eyes of the average man.

Fresh air fills his lungs
with promise and hope.

Wishes wander around
the streets of his mind,
looking for a brand-new outlook on life.

Making him travel to new places,
wherever his imagination conjures up,
he goes for Grace.

The Grace I know walks with two legs,
and reaches everyone in her path.

February 2021

It Can Only Break Me
Monday, February 1, 2021

When Reality pricks at me,
it's a needle to gather the blood
modern medicine needs.

How much to keep me safe
from mental illness and myself?

Take everything
you need from me Reality.

Whatever it takes to bring me back
to a home I can remember.

Home isn't what it once was,
isn't safe,
isn't what I remembered.

Home has become a place
where my mind tricks me.

The loved side of me left,
and fear is what's left.

Reality left me frantic,
searching for answers
to questions which don't exist.

Responsibility became my undertaking,
the consequences are mine to take,
no matter what they are.

Reality is a pill to take
to end the fear,
to make me remember who to hold dear.

Reality could try its worst,
but it couldn't break my heart,
my relationships.

You Can Get Back Up
Wednesday, February 3, 2021

Tragedy- a stumble
with no ability to get back up.

No one's around to lend a hand,
I find my own arms
unable to pick you up.

Helpless, I can only hand
you the encouragement
to get up on your own.

It's heartbreaking how I wish
I could do something to help
you move the world.

There are times when you fall,
and no one can help you up.

The strength must come from within yourself.

The biggest tragedy is the limbo-state
you find yourself stuck in.

Questioning if you can feel normal once more.

Hang in there, it takes time, it will get better.

The only problem is, no one knows when,
but if you keep at it, it will be okay.

While I can't explain life and it's complexities.
I can only explain me, how it's a miracle I'm alive.
I don't know how to fix people,
I only know how to speak to them.

Be careful with your words
because you don't know
when your words could count the most.

A simple hello can make a person's morning.
At times, it's essential to tell someone,
"You're not hopeless, you're not a tragedy."

Before Anyone Else
Monday, February 8, 2021

Dead friendship dreams remind me
of the troubles I left behind.

What a blessing to form new friendships.
Because the greatest of friends
will lift you up when you fall,
rather than drag you through the mud.

When getting caught up in memories,
don't forget the moment you're living in.
The past is dead and gone,
and there's nothing you can do to fix past mishaps.

Past opportunities- lost,
but the future will bring along new ones.
New people will come along,
some will be for you,
some will be against you.
You don't have to allow anyone
in your life who will bring you down.

Most empowering, love yourself first.

If You Can Find It

Tuesday, February 16, 2021

A decade passed,
my head was in the clouds,
fueled by hopes and dreams.

Today I'm dedicated
to setting lofty goals,
and achieving each one.

On occasion,
my head drifts back to those dreams
and I find myself living them.

Whether known, or unknown,
I have words in the world.

I'm committed,
despite any judgment,
I carry on,
I keep writing.

My dreams may not be
what I thought they would be.

I'm the stubborn girl
who has everything
she wanted out of life.

After getting everything I wanted,
I found more.

A bottomless well of inspiration,
a breath-taking sip of hope.

The water is clear,
will not muddy,
pure and ready to drink.

So help yourself to the well.

Gravity

Monday, February 22, 2021

I'm moving on from deaf ears
and empty chair audiences.
The empty effort is no more.
I'm moving forward,
walking down easier avenues.

I will find the weight of my words,
the gravity of my achievements.
My hope is to change the heart of man,
to ease his aching soul.
As each man has the potential
to save our dying earth,
if we award them the occasion.

These are the abilities of humanity,
the powers we possess.
To speak until we lose our voices,
then find a listening ear.

It only takes two to change the world,
one to speak of invention,
and the other a hand in creation.

Only Aurora Knows
Wednesday, February 24, 2021

The world stopped,
while gaining momentum,
stars crashed into the earth for me.

I saw so much more than black,
I saw stars of each color.

My awareness was amethyst
in an array of ways,
gorgeous, you could say.

I wish I saw myself this way.

Enamored by Aurora's
earthly nightlight,
I wonder if I could be her light.

Could I be capable of lighting
the room I walk in?

Could I be a purple glow
to catch your eye?

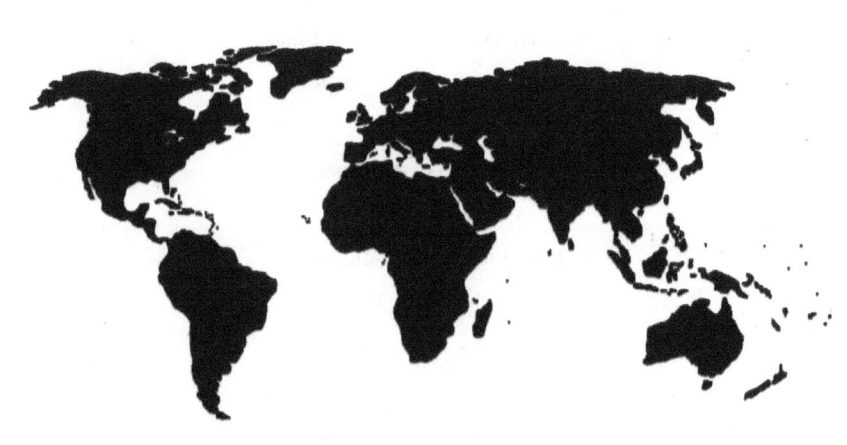

March 2021

Stay With Me
Monday, March 1, 2021

Trying my hardest
to ease humanity's unseen illnesses.

Unsure of whether I'm making a difference or not,
I put myself out into the world of sickness.

I push past my fears
to find healing isn't so far from us.

Some have to leap through hoops to get help.

Fairness isn't awarded
to everyone without a support system.

It's wise for the ill to know their options,
learn how to stay in a good mental-space,
to be an example for the less fortunate.

No one knows the power a person can possess
if you don't stick around long enough to see it.

So when their life is at risk,
I'll remind them of their strength,
I will not let them down!

My Dominion Is My Worth

Tuesday, March 9, 2021

The world exists for me
and each rational creature in it.

I've built my world
in this messy house of mine;
a writer's trade,
a crafter's heart,
an engineer's home.

The idea in my mind telling me,
I do make a difference.

Who can stop me from success?

No one but myself,
getting in my own way.

My worth, my dominion,
doesn't count on anyone but me.

A new question is,
how do I get out of my dominion,
and into the universe?

I can't stop wanting more,
donating more,
taking less.

I'm forevermore looking to expand
my world,
my worth,
and my dominion.

I Will Achieve
Tuesday, March 16, 2021

For the first time in forever,
I felt joy:
A quiet miracle,
alone, in my mind.
Family, a couple's comradery,
a feeling of togetherness.

My wishes fade so far
in the moment of affection.

Everything I have is my focus.

To hold tight,
and let my heart wander to you,
as it does.

To let each dream of mine
come true in my own time.

At times, one person,
and a second of faith,
is the push needed to achieve.

Trembling, She Forgave

Tuesday, March 23, 2021

My heart, crushed by bitter ugliness,
who took the form of a familiar person.

A friend called him brother,
I called him stranger as his hands
slithered where they didn't belong.

Forgiveness?
What could it be?
I tried to be friendly
as this joke backfired on me.

Crushed, and trying to gather myself,
making sense of the situation.
Too young to understand,
too young to consent
to such an atrocious act.

How to forgive?
How to forgive?

Time changes everything,
through trauma
and flashbacks.

I look at the past through a lens,
as if it happened to another person.
Would I tell this child to forgive?

Never!
I would tell her to let
time heal her wounds,
but forgiveness is for
the greatest of friends and family.

Small View Of Mine

Wednesday, March 31, 2021

I pick up my head to see
everything surrounding me.
My eyes soak in this tiny town,
and its cold spring splendor.

I think about God's perspective,
how vast His gaze must be.
A landscape of a mountain,
could be but hills to Him.

My singular two-eyed view
only has one story to tell,
but God has millions-
how can I compete?

I can't-
but I have my own story
to finish telling, to finish living.

The story of my life, God has written
in His grand perspective
and I'm fixed on writing this.

April 2021

Understanding Freedom
Monday, April 5, 2021

Bound to everything you own and love.
A home, a family might bind you.

Freedom is a choice so honest,
we're even free to redefine free.
Freedom is a mentality,
understand it's an exchange.

Freedom does not come
without complexities.
It's a well oiled machine
exchanging time and labor
for the opportunity to be free.

Home-bound isn't the worst you can be,
but to say you're not free
because of a complexity,
is the worst sort of mistake.

Everything

Wednesday, April 14, 2021

Nature is the servant of man,
providing earth to plant,
providing everything.

Everything originates in nature,
our shelter,
our homes made of clay brick,
cement, wood, nails, and stone.

Nature provided each material for us,
for our enrichment, and our freedom.

It is the obligation of each man
living in human nature
to preserve nature as he chooses.

The blessings we don't see,
occur in nature.

Set your miseries to the side,
and be grateful
for what nature has provided.

Don't Give In
Tuesday, April 20, 2021

American media headlines
play the world's worst game
of telephone with the public.

The truth doesn't need
a telephone to speak.
It needs eyes willing
to read entire articles.

Headlines lie to grab
your attention,
then pull you in
for gossips full of lies.

All before you've had
the chance to read for yourself.

Careful,
or you'll become
the echo chamber
of telephone truth.

Wisdom Vs Knowledge

Thursday, April 29, 2021

A humbled wisdom,
holds a prehension of the world.

Knowledge holds its pride,
its expectation is one
of blatant obligation.

A clear burden
on the shoulders of men,
one wisdom seems to ease.

Let knowledge enrich you
but let wisdom fine-tune you
till you're a quality artisan.

Knowledge can't teach
what the wisdom
of common sense can deliver.

May 2021

Sleep On It
Tuesday, May 4, 2021

Whispers crackle in the back of my mind
like a withering candle,
a wick burning to its impending end.

A pillow of thoughts to sink my head into
while I sort through withering whispers.

A blanket of questions in mind,
they drape over me,
holding me down.

The questions no one can answer,
stay unknown as I
search my mind for a solution.

Blow out your crackling candle,
and pray for a sound pillow tonight.
There's only one way to find your answers.

It's Not Coming Back

Wednesday, May 12, 2021

Pain, a creature,
creeping in and out of our bodies.

He creeps into our mental space,
leaving blanks to fill.

A creature like amnesia
erases any memory of pain.

I can not imagine why.

Can not imagine
such a creature's embrace,
but he's had his hold on me.

Sucked me in to this world of skepticism,
where nothing is real,
question everything. Reality is gone.

Drat Hit The Rabbit

Tuesday, May 25, 2021

Chasing the rabbit's wish,
down each hole he dug.

Dead-end dreamers
chasing rabbit's wishes
find themselves in the dark.

A severed foot is what's found,
a symbol of good luck
at the cost of the rabbit's life.

It was unknown, how,
the rabbit is luckier alive,
in one piece.

Soul and spirit, divine-
is the rabbit's living gift.

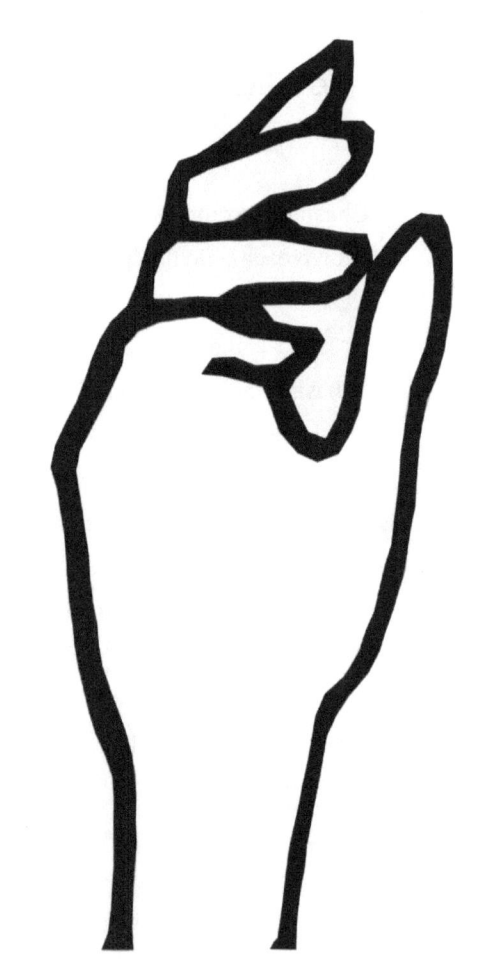

June 2021

Feel Your Fate
Monday, June 7, 2021

Blank canvas and I,
we have quite the relationship.

Found myself blind,
using my fingers to read
the texture on the walls.

How much more blank canvas could I be?

Faceless, mirrored, I stood,
trying to recognize myself.
Blank canvas was all I could see.

In a panic, I ask myself,
"Who am I?"
I am faceless, blank canvas.

Read the walls of acceptance.

Take Care

Friday, June 18, 2021

It's a sad world full of sad people.
Everyone can commiserate in sadness.

Reach out with your sorrows,
outstretch a hand and ask.

The power to say no
to negative thought
is in your hands.

Fingertips to slip through-
don't lose your hope,
don't lose yourself.

Clear Your Mind
Thursday, June 24, 2021

Find peace within yourself,
brew some coffee,
watch the steam rise.

End personal battles,
pour yourself a cup,
wait for it to cool.

Tea isn't for everyone to spill,
quiet your mind and mouth.

Focus on yourself,
tune everything out.

Open your mind,
don't think,
take a sip.

Take the time
to be transparent.

Silent

Monday, June 28, 2021

Disconnected,
counting the metaphoric miles
between my world and me.

Struck by the reality
of complete strangers surrounding me.

Disconnect,
don't understand anyone-
but be there,
to be...

Exist for what?
To be me,
or something,
or nothing,
how am I to know?
I've become lost in my existence,
what have I been created for?

Once, I knew the answer,
had a super singular view on life,
well, my view has strayed.

I've humbled myself.
My problems became menial,
and I can't bring myself to care
about the menial any longer.

The world can take my menial life,
and I'd be none the wiser,
as I have nothing left to offer.

I continue to breathe,
but can't understand why.

I don't belong here,
don't know why,
but I continue to be.

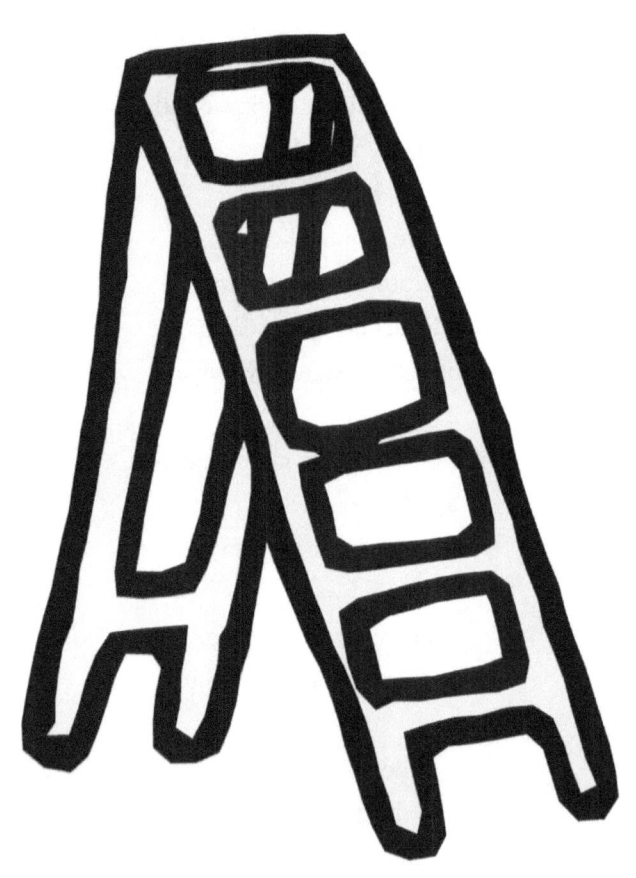

July 2021

<u>Casting Shadows</u>
Thursday, July 1, 2021

Confidence is crucial
to cracking cowardice.

Fight your fears
to climb the ladder.

Climb to find your lost character
-to find yourself.

Inch out into the sun
or stay hidden in the dark.

Darkness only knows
the light can cast its shadow.

Follow in the footsteps
of shadowy greatness,
and let the sun create you.

Don't compare yourself
to other creations,
you're the only person
in your particular position.

How is greatness achieved?
How are you to know
until you try?

Work
Wednesday, July 7, 2021

Humanity dreams of the multitudes-
healthier lives, peace, occupation, retirement.

We dream of what's around the corner,
what we can build for years to come.

Execution is the tricky part,
and the willingness to move on
after striking a stumbling block.

How do you cope?

Do you move on
and try to step over
this block as you build?

Ignorance creates weakness,
keep trying till you stumble no more.

Self Doubt Is A Sickness

Wednesday, July 14, 2021

A question, a thousand times a day,
vanishes when it counts.

A question collision,
causes self-doubt.

Ask it when it counts.
Ask it, when it, counts.

Self-doubt creates a trap,
caged inside our own minds.

A fear of failure,
a fear of success.
A fear of death,
a fear of living.

A fear of the unknown, living,
somewhere in between.

Between failure and success,
alive, but not living.

Where You Belong

Thursday, July 22, 2021

We're drifting on a ship,
unaware of who will float
in and out of our lives.

Question who to keep close,
and who to let coast into the distance.

Drifting through this life,
you will meet millions.
There are a million mouths
to speak their peace about you.
Yet not a single voice matters
unless it matters to you.

You'll have your own opinions,
you'll hold your tongue,
you'll spill your guts.

You'll learn about this world,
how to handle yourself,
how to handle others.
How to anchor yourself.

Was It Worth It?

Monday, July 26, 2021

We own not a single item in this life,
we only rent and borrow until we die.

Arrogance doesn't
overshadow benevolent acts.

No throne can make your life,
or worldly possessions
worth more than mine.

You are not superior to me,
or anyone I know.

Possessions are not
more precious than people.

Pride can be such
a malevolent device,
it can be willing to kill
to keep its dignity.

August 2021

Willing To Learn
Wednesday, August 4, 2021

On occasion, we have to
surrender to our circumstance
and give up with grace.

Admit defeat,
heal your broken heart,
new beginnings.

You have the choice
to put the past behind you.
The choice to empty your picture frames
and put new memories inside.

Everyone in this world idles lost,
sifting through what to keep,
and what to toss.

What will you miss?
What can you buy brand new?
What should be tossed to the trash?

Some objects stay missing forevermore,
some objects are lessons learned.
Some lessons are meant to pass
on to the next student.

New Beginnings
Wednesday, August 11, 2021

Hope comes in many forms
-a spark, a firefly.

A small something to light up your life,
to keep you occupied in troubled times.

Hope does not wander aimless,
it targets those at risk of losing faith.

It pulls you out of misery
in the most miraculous ways.

Hope has a way of making life okay.

Believe In Yourself

Friday, August 20, 2021

Faith is the freedom to believe
in something or someone,
anyone or anything.

Trust takes a leap of faith,
confide in who you can.

Pride pulls you down to earth,
or sends you skyrocketing
into outer space.

The spirit of a thriving character is courageous.

Don't let your weakness kill your spirit,
let your strength keep you confident.

Be brave, without worry,
let your intuition lead the way.

Be Your Own Bounty

Wednesday, August 25, 2021

Minuscule miracles
catch our eyes each day,
keep us moving.

No questions,
struggles,
operating order,
and we're happy.

Just getting by,
just drifting,
mini miracles make you.

You shut the door
on a predestined fate,
exceeded expectations.

There's the small matter
of presumptions, no matter at all.

You weren't born in bounty,
but you earned it.

Let Us Stop Pretending
Thursday, August 26, 2021

I don't know who God is,
no matter how much I try.

I don't know of heaven or hell,
only earth.

My place is not to judge
a heathen or a believer.

As much as I try to understand what's beyond my reach,
my reach only extends to my fingertips.

Oh, how I'd love to tell you
I know each answer.

I only have opinions on the matter,
many questions of my own.
Some about suffering,
some about emptiness,
many about how to overcome your ailments.

So, I sit and pray for some answers,
but my prayers turn out to be deep sighs for humanity.
So much I can't understand,
I can't find the words to express my gratefulness,
or my hopes for humankind.

I get up off my knees and understand,
everything is out of my control.

I hear everything is in God's hands,
bothersome to believe.
I don't believe God acts this way,
I believe free will kills His control.

I Hope So

Tuesday, August 31, 2021

Nothing's on my mind,
an existential problem.

I've come to the conclusion,
division is inevitable...
Sad.

Politics appear to worm their way into everything.

How do I explain personal choice,
a love of self?

Everyone only tries to do what's best
for the love of self, then everyone else.

Understanding humanity is hard for some
-but I understand the love of self.

Being kind to everyone else is problematic for most,
but I find myself caving in to respect.
Instead of being problematic,
I find myself silent.

Robbed of my voice. . .

Speechless at the sounds of so much disrespect,
and how do I cope?

I shut myself out of these four walls,
and watch the real world keep moving.

The question is, am I moving with it?

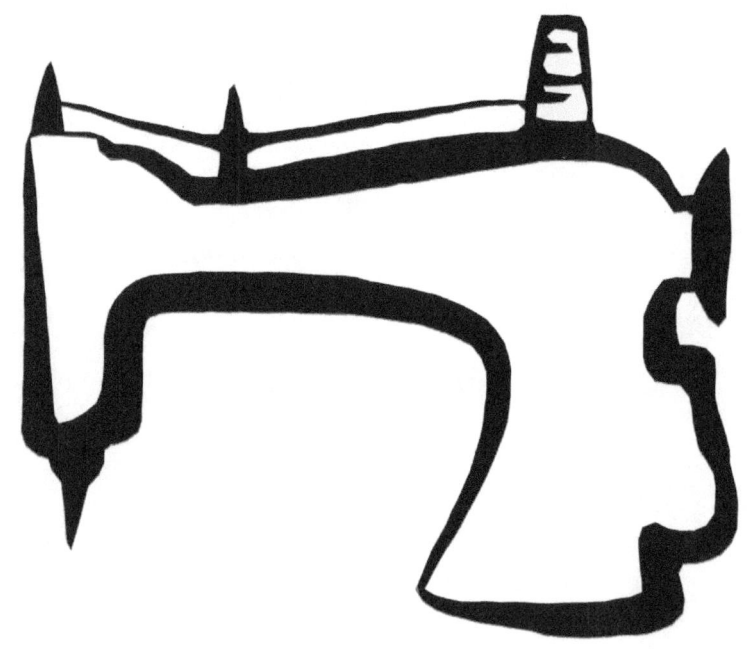

September 2021

I Don't Owe The World A Thing
Wednesday, September 8, 2021

Hands deep into the fabric of my mindset,
I pick up two pieces and feed them through.

I sat in front of my machine,
expecting myself to improve the world.

Focused on nothing other than
the threads of time connecting us.
What time is it? What day is it? I don't even know.
Threads, torn.

I keep tossing scraps to the side
and sewing my spirit into everything.

Slow, I start to unravel.
My well-being becomes unbound
scraps of fabric spread across the floor.

Thinking -anything the world needs- I have it.

Stage Three, Wondering What's To Come?
Wednesday, September 15, 2021

Frequently I see my life flicker before my eyes.

I can't seem to find a phase, a place in the past to call a stage.
I realize, today and yesterday
are the only two stages I've been through in life.

The moment, the present, and the past,
have been both harsh and helpful.

How can I? How could I make myself more clear?

I'm swimming, barely breathing, coming up for air.
I take it in, let it go, take it in, let go of the past,
and at times- everyone in it.

Dead or alive, I honor the memory of melancholy or peace.

It seems I'm secretly sad -thinking of what I miss-
forever mourning memories, acceptable or atrocious.

Trapped in the moment, unable
to travel back through time, or forward to the future.

Everything
Monday, September 20, 2021

I want to make you understand,
to make you question,
to inspire, to be...

A light in the dark, a spark,
the illuminated light bulb above your head.

An idea,
a new beginning,
hope, logic,
a new way of thinking.

Carefree,
a walk in the park,
a fresh start.

A clean slate,
a new state of mind,
a sight to the blind,
a sound to the deaf.

If only I could be.

Roman Empires
Thursday, September 23, 2021

Perspective in a pinch,
what would you see?

The rambling girl,
or the messiah I claimed to be.

Step inside my mind, while I step outside.

Stories about how I broke-
a divine gesture, a sacred whisper.

No hints to this secret,
only injury to memory.

The miracle of medicine,
the pills I swallow save
and kill me many ways.

What can I do? How can I cope?

Say goodbye to a clear mind,
and move on.

October 2021

The Secrets You Will Keep
Thursday, October 7, 2021

My perspective of God is now, so vast,
my narrow mind, a thing of the past.

A singular view
sitting in this pew.

God isn't who I thought
-isn't who I was taught.

Scripture is seeing through the eye of a needle
into the past of Jesus-God and the steeple.

The fundamental secrets I keep
of a God so deep
are not the same
as the creator you claim.

The Almighty of Black and White is plain as day
-every single Sad and Happy shade of Gray.

How do I show you what I see
without your judgment passed on me?

Family
Wednesday, October 20, 2021

My strings tethered
tight to a violin
humming a familiar song.

I'm your strings attached,
a forget-me-not,
a mousy ear of reason.

You are the violin,
I'm tethered tight to you.
You are familiar.

I Am Not Him
Wednesday, October 27, 2021

Lost myself in the midst
of the mayhem called my mind.

Carried up in a windstorm of word and thought.

"Who am I?" I ask myself,
trying to conjure something existential,
but crisis is what comes up, confusion.

When I couldn't find myself,
the only one left was You.

A name I could claim with clumsy confidence,
but I'll keep Him anonymous.

I stuck with this toy-train of thought, full of conviction.

"I AM!" I declare, "I AM!"
I am simply sad, sick, and desperate for help.

All I wanted was to be more.

November 2021

From Anxiety
Tuesday, November 9, 2021

Thoughts spiral above my head,
a twister of chaos
destroying everything in its path.

Hands shaking,
holding tight to reality.

I must face this frightening fit of terror alone,
and walk with the chaos above my head.

The burden to bear,
of an unbalanced brain is bitter,
a cold taste of fear,
a hard swallow.

Wanting,
very much,
to be free.

Until You Look Closely
Wednesday, November 17, 2021

Confusion, balled up
and twisted to untangle.

Hands woven
within the wires,
bound to break
this mental clutter.

Arms attached to scissors-
cut through each wire,
string and rope tangled together.

Anything can be accomplished
with the correct tools.

Even feeble minds are capable
of miraculous crafts.

The talent behind
the tattered and torn
ropes, wires and strings
is unknown.

I'm Speaking To You

Monday, November 29, 2021

I am a figment of my own fantasy,
I dreamt myself up,
fabricated myself.

An authentic being,
illuminated by the inspiration
of everything I see, hear,
touch and consume.

In my past, I was blank as the pages I fill,
today I create life out of ink and squiggles.

Are you alive today?
Are you hanging by an inch of what I say?

Listen, my heart is empty of anguish,
it's been poured out on paper.

I'm alive today,
even if my body has decayed.

But Myself
Tuesday, November 30, 2021

A somber soliloquy,
spoken to a room full of suffering patients.

An invisible illness,
identified by unusual behavior.

Hospitalized for being unable to function.

A simple soliloquy of confident contemplation.

Not a soul understood the pressure
to be positive in a pessimistic place.

Parading myself in misery
and the powerful desire
to triumph over this disorder.

My mind wandered to grant my wishes,
even if they were hallucinations.

I've spoken to the dead in the depths of my mind,
took advice from no one.

December 2021

I Found My Paper Doll
Tuesday, December 7, 2021

Love notes to myself.

An abstract admirer
creates a secret confidence.

Notes none would speak,
words of love, enchantment.

Everything I wished for,
in paper form.

If he, a paper doll, were authentic
-rather than an extension of myself-
I'd be overflowing with encouragement.

I've Witnessed It
Wednesday, December 15, 2021

Take a wild trip into the unknown,
a peak inside a dreamer's heart.

I'm grateful to have my tongue
to speak of fate and creation.

Creation beyond an earthly thought
conjured up by simple men.

Architects, engineers, and physicists
toil to complete a vision of aimless dreams.

There's something magical
about these men
who bring their dreams to life.

The imagination, the innovation,
of dreams come to life
is sensational to see.

John's Symbolic Vision

Wednesday, December 22, 2021

When we rise again,
the poets will be
the first to face East.

Our rising Sun
will rescue us once more.

Creation will flourish
with our vision,
we will have insight
into nature.

The ebbs and flows
of our imaginations
will be free
to paint the earth.

It will become
our canvas
to adorn
as He once did.

She Never Did

Thursday, December 30, 2021

I have no explanations,
no theories.
-Fate is a mystery
of death and misery.

Beauty defined it,
a state of mind,
sorrow's kind.

Grief idles in absolutes,
but nothing is certain
except for denial, its impact -a burden.

Fate handed Beauty the hindrance
of addiction and denial.
Then tossed her into the earth
to wither, then rebirth.

www.ingramcontent.com/pod-product-compliance
Lightning Source LLC
Chambersburg PA
CBHW020611220526
45463CB00006B/2554